GRIP

Redstone Press
7a St Lawrence Terrace, London W10 5SU
www.redstonepress.co.uk

GRIP was first published in 2000
by Morning Star Publications, Polygon and Redstone Press

This edition 2008

Layout: Kim McKinney
Production: Tim Chester
Printed in China by C & C Offset Printing

ISBN 978-1-870003-14-8

A CIP record for this book is available from the British Library

October 2008.

To Helen

♡ Happy Birthday   ♡

P.S. I hope you   Lots of love
find this inspiring   from Emma
but not disturbing!   x x x

EQUATION TO EXPLAIN YOUR EXPULSION, EXCLUSION AND CONDEMNATION.

IF :

A = THINGS THAT MEAN NOTHING

AND

B = THINGS THAT MEAN NOTHING
TO YOU

AND

C = THINGS THAT MEAN EVERYTHING

AND

D = THINGS THAT MEAN EVERYTHING
TO YOU

THEN :

$A = D$ AND $B = C$

COSTUMES
FOR HIRE

ANIMALS

BALOU
BROWN BEAR
BUMBLE BEE
BUNGLE
CAMEL (2 MAN)
CATS
CHICKENS
CROCODILE
DINOSAURS
DOGS
DUCK
ELEPHANTS
EMU
FLEA
FROG
FOX
GORILLAS
HIPPO
HONEY BEAR
LIONS
LION CUB
PANDAS
PANTO COW
PANTO HORSE
PARROT
PENGUIN
RABBITS
REINDEER (2 MAN)
SLUG
WHALE

ERAS

GANGSTERS
FORTIES
ROCK 'N ROLL
TEDDY BOYS
HIPPIES
SIXTIES
SEVENTIES

CHILDRENS' CHARACTERS

ALICE
ANDY PANDY
LOOBY LOO
BUTTONS
CAPTAIN HOOK
CINDERELLA
CLOWNS
DENNIS
DINO
DOROTHY
DUCK
DWARFS
FAIRIES
FAIRY GODMOTHER
FRED
BARNEY
WILMA
SMURFS
HARLEQUIN
JESTER
KING & QUEEN OF HEARTS
MAD HATTER
MISS MUFFET
PANTO DAME
PINOCHIO
TIN MAN
TWEEDLE DUM
TWEEDLE DEE
WIZARD

FAMOUS

BEATLES   ROBIN
BLUES BROTHERS
CHAPLIN
CLEOPATRA
ELVIS
GARY GLITTER
HITLER
MARILYN MONROE
DARTH VADAR
BATMAN

NATIONALITIES

- ARAB
- CAN CAN
- CHINESE
- COMIC SCOT
- FRENCH MAIDS
- GENDARME
- GREEK FEMALE
- GYPSY
- HAREM GIRLS
- HUNGARIAN
- MEXICAN
- SPANISH
- SULTAN
- TYROLIAN MALE
- TYROLIAN FEMALE
- UNCLE SAM

HORROR

- DEVIL
- DRACULA
- EXECUTIONER
- FRANKENSTEIN
- GRIM REAPER
- MORITICIA
- MUMMY
- SCARY ELEPHANT
- SKELETON
- WITCHES

UNIFORMS

- AMERICAN COP
- BROWNIE
- BIGGLES
- CONVICT
- DRUM MAJOR
- JOCKEY
- PRISON GAURD
- POSTMAN
- INQUISITOR
- LEGIONNAIRE

- JANITOR
- CANADIAN MOUNTIE
- R.A.F.
- SCHOOL GIRLS
- SCHOOL BOYS
- SCHOOL MASTER
- UNION SOLDIER

OTHERS

- BABY BOY
- BABY GIRL
- BANANA
- CRIPPLE
- CAVEMAN
- HUNCHBACK
- ESMERALDA
- PIRATES
- RING MASTER
- SOFA
- SAUCY W.P.C.
- RETARD
- TRAMP

PERIOD

- HENRY VIII
- ELIZABETH I
- CHARLES III
- EDWARD I
- CHARLES IV
- NAPOLEON

CHRISTMAS

- SANTA
- SEXY SANTA
- PRIEST
- VICAR
- NUNS   CHOIRBOY

SUPREME BEINGS

- MOTHER NATURE
- GOD
- STAR TREK CHARACTERS

WESTERN

- COWBOY
- COWGIRL
- INDIAN BRAVE
- INDIAN SQUAW

NEED ACCESSORIES?   WE SELL:

BANNERS - BEARDS - BODY PARTS - BOAS - FLAGS - BUNTING -
HATS - MOUSTACHES - MAKE UP - MASKS - FACE PAINTS - HAIRSPRAY
WIGS - WINGS - BOW TIES - GLOVES

WE HAVE MANY MORE COSTUMES IN STOCK
FOR YOU TO SEE AND TRY ON.

COME AND VISIT US ON THE FIRST FLOOR

BITTER-TASTING FRUITS OF NEGLECT:

YOU AND YOUR GOOD LADY GO ON HOLIDAY TO NEW ZEALAND FOR 2 MONTHS AND NEGLECT TO MAKE PROVISION FOR YOUR HOUSEPLANTS TO BE WATERED.

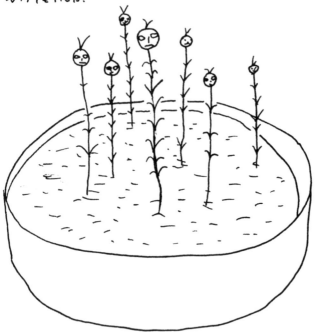

DISCONCERTINGLY THEY NOT ONLY SURVIVE BUT BEAR FRUIT (WHICH IS BITTER-TASTING). THIS FRUIT BORN OF NEGLECT IS AKIN (YOU COME TO SUSPECT) TO YOUR DAUGHTER'S ANTI-SOCIAL BEHAVIOUR.

FARMER TRIES TO RETRIEVE
TRACTOR TYRE FROM AROUND
DINOSAUR'S NECK.

WILL YOU PROVIDE ASSISTANCE?

WHAT'S THIS ?
- IT'S A SYMBOL

WHAT DO IT MEAN ?

- IT MEAN 'DARREN IS A FUCKING
                          MORON'

(LONG SILENCE, DARREN THINKS)

NO IT DOESN'T ?
- YES IT DOES

I'm so lucky   I'm so lucky
I'm so lucky   I'm so lucky

what   a
beautiful plant

I hope they let me keep it

COMPLETE ABSENCE OF TYPEFACE

NO A's   NO B's   NO C's   NO D's

NO E's   NO F's   NO G's   NO H's

NO I's   NO J's   NO K's   NO L's

NO M's   NO N's   NO O's   NO P's

NO Q's   NO R's   NO S's   NO T's

NO U's   NO V's   NO W's   NO X's

NO Y's   NO Z's, NO .'s, ,'s, !'s, OR ?'s

AND NO 1's, 2's, 3's, 4's, 5's, 6's, 7's, 8's, 9's, OR 0's.

WISE OLD OWL
THICK AS SHIT

THE MAN WHO SAID "THERE IS NOTHING TO FEAR" IS MADE TO EAT HIS WORDS (ONE LETTER AT A TIME).

NESTING

WHERE DO THE SEAGULLS NEST?

— THE SEAGULLS NEST ON THE CLIFFS.

WHERE DO THE LARKS NEST?

— THE LARKS NEST IN THE TREES.

WHERE DO THE OWLS NEST?

— THE OWLS NEST IN THE BARN.

WHERE DO THE EAGLES NEST.

— THE EAGLES NEST IN THE GRAND CANYON.

WHERE DO THE ⬭ MONKIES NEST?

— THE MONKIES NEST AT THE ZOO.

WHERE DO THE FLEAS NEST?

— THE FLEAS NEST IN YOUR HAIR.

AND WHERE DO YOU NEST?

— I USED TO NEST WITH MY MUM
AND DAD UNTIL THEY CHUCKED
ME OUT AND NOW I LIVE WITH
MY BROTHER SUSAN.

PRIZEGIVING IS INTERRUPTED BY LUNATIC

ORGY IS
INTERRUPTED
BY EARTHQUAKE

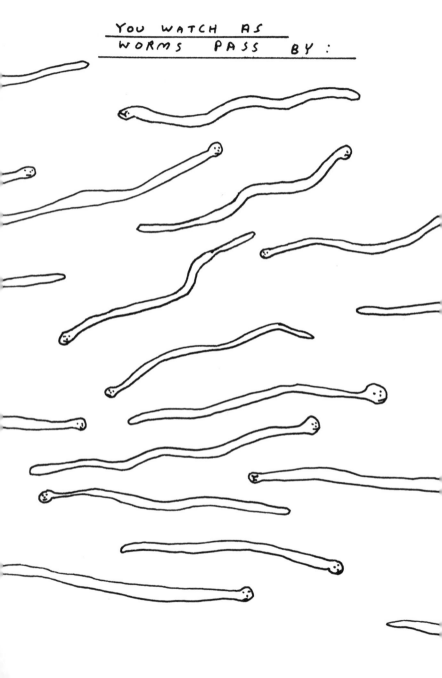

FACTORY WHICH MAKES SNOWMEN OWNED
AND RUN BY MR J. FROST

MRS. ACORN

MR. ACORN

ASSESSMENT

1A. WHAT WORRIES YOU ABOUT MRS. ACORN ?

1B. WHAT WORRIES YOU ABOUT MR. ACORN ?

2A. WHAT ENDEARS YOU TO MRS. ACORN ?

2B. WHAT ENDEARS YOU TO MR. ACORN ?

3A. UPON WHICH ASPECTS OF MRS. ACORN HAVE YOU NO OPINION?

3B. UPON WHICH ASPECTS OF MR. ACORN HAVE YOU NO OPINION?

4A. IF I TOLD YOU I WAS GOING TO TIE MRS. ACORN TO A CHAIR AND GIVE HER ELECTRIC SHOCKS WOULD YOU TRY TO STOP ME ?

YES / NO

4B. IF I TOLD YOU I WAS GOING TO TIE MR. ACORN TO A CHAIR AND GIVE HIM ELECTRIC SHOCKS WOULD YOU TRY TO STOP ME ?

YES / NO

5. DO YOU THINK IT'S CRUEL TO GIVE FUNNY-LOOKING PEOPLE ELECTRIC SHOCKS ?

YES / NO

LAND USED BY MASTURBATORS

(RUN FROM)

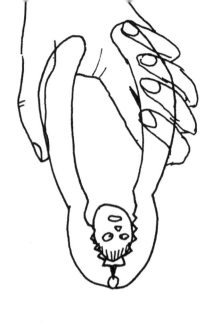

TRUE LIGHTS	FALSE LIGHTS
DAYLIGHT	LIGHT- EMITTING SPAGHETTI
LAMPLIGHT	BIG MATCH HIGHLIGHTS
MOONLIGHT	OTHER HIGHLIGHTS
STARLIGHT	(PARTICULARLY THOSE
HEADLIGHT	PETAINING TO YOUR
TRAFFIC LIGHT	LIFE AND THINGS YOU
TORCH LIGHT	HAVE DONE)
FIRE LIGHT	
CANDLE LIGHT	MARLBORO LIGHTS
DISCO LIGHT	
LANDING LIGHT	
SAFETY LIGHT	
SEARCH LIGHT	
STREET LIGHT	
NEON LIGHT	
NIGHT LIGHT	

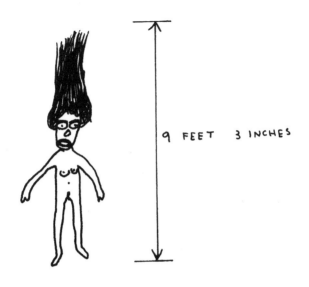

9 FEET 3 INCHES

THIS WHORE

PRICES

TALK AT HER... £ 10
TALK TO HER (HER TALKING ALSO)............... £ 11
TOUCH HAIR... £ 10
LICK HAIR.. £ 11
RIDE ELEPHANT WITH HER........................ £ 100
RIDE ELEPHANT ALONE.............................. £ 11
LOOK AT MINGE.. £ 11
LOOK AT ELEPHANT'S MINGE....................... £ 10

    ALL OTHER TYPES OF SEX FORBIDDEN

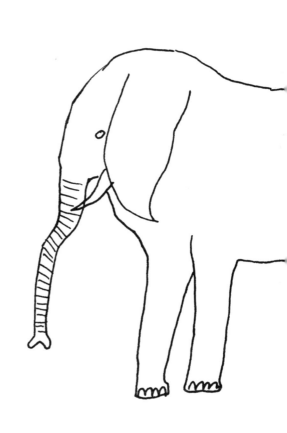

NON - BELIEVER   BELIEVER

SWEARING CONTEST

LOSING —
BLOODY FINALIST

CHAMPION OF
THE FUCKING
WORLD

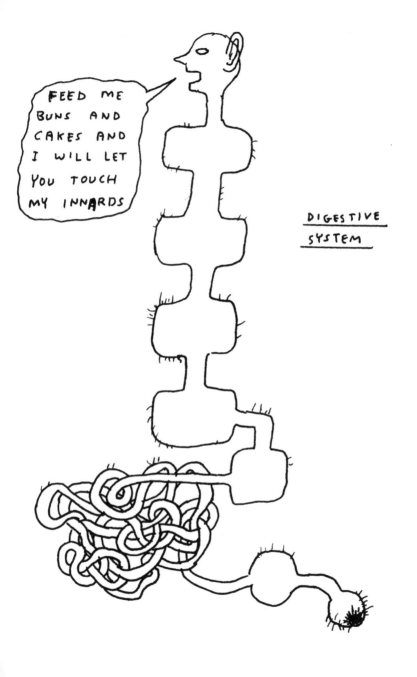

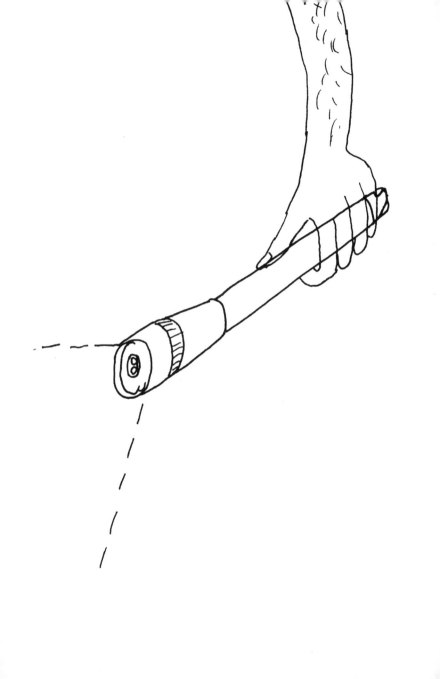

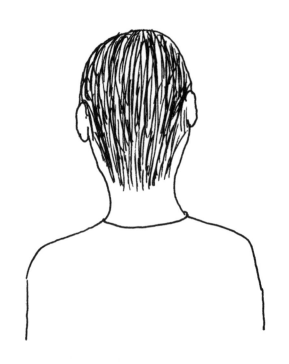

A DESCRIPTION OF THE GESTURE I AM
MAKING BEHIND YOUR BACK:

I AM HOPPING ON ONE LEG. MY
RAISED FOOT IS BARE (EXCEPT FOR NAIL VARNISH)
; THE SUPPORTING FOOT IS IN A WELLINGTON
BOOT. MY STOMACH IS UNDULATING LIKE A
BELLY-DANCER. I AM WEARING A DRESS.
ONE ARM IS STIFF WITH HAND FLACID;
ONE ARM IS WAVING ABOUT WILDLY;
MY HEAD IS MOVING FROM SIDE TO SIDE;
MY TONGUE IS STUCK OUT AND WIGGLING;
MY EYES ARE CROSSED; I AM GROANING.

BRUTAL TRUTHS:

IN REALITY ANGELS LOOK LIKE GIANT INSECT

EMOTIONALLY, I WISH TO
BE REPRESENTED BY THIS IMAGE:

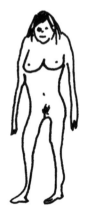

SPIRITUALLY, I WISH TO BE
REPRESENTED BY THIS IMAGE:

WHEN I REACHED 13 YEARS
OF AGE MY BODY STARTED
TO CHANGE......

THE NUTCASE

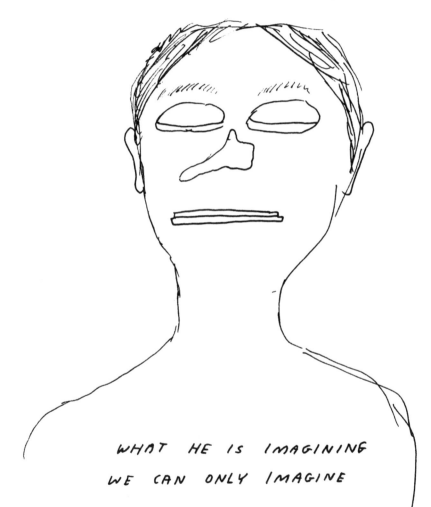

WHAT HE IS IMAGINING
WE CAN ONLY IMAGINE

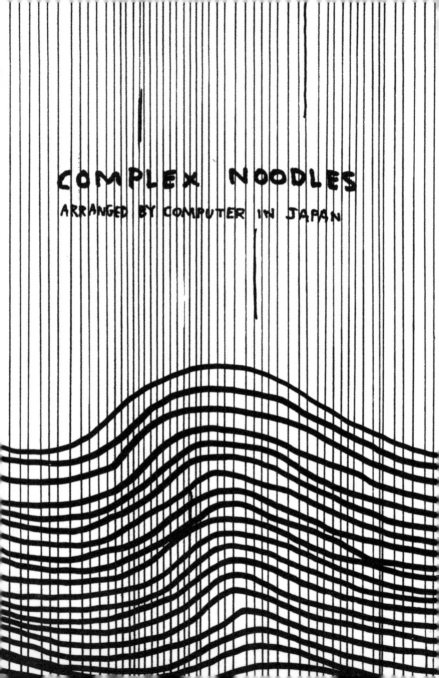

MUSHROOMS

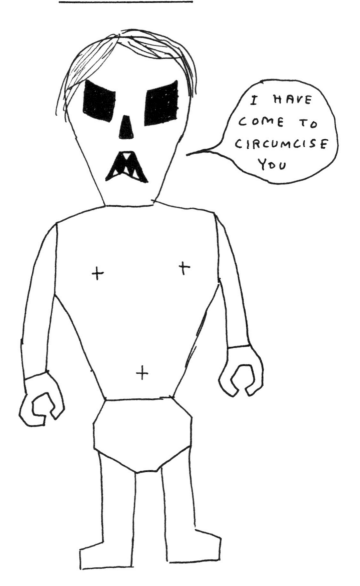

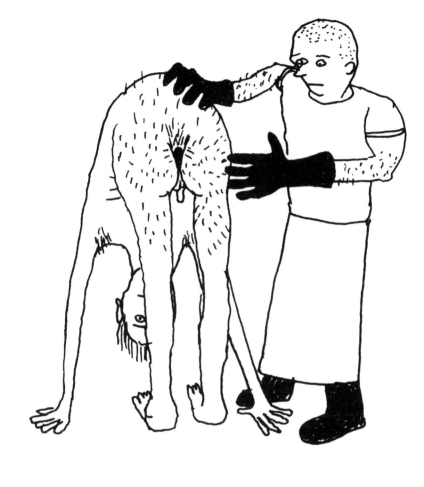

THE GRIM TASK
TO RETRIEVE THE
LOST ITEM
a silver pocket-watch

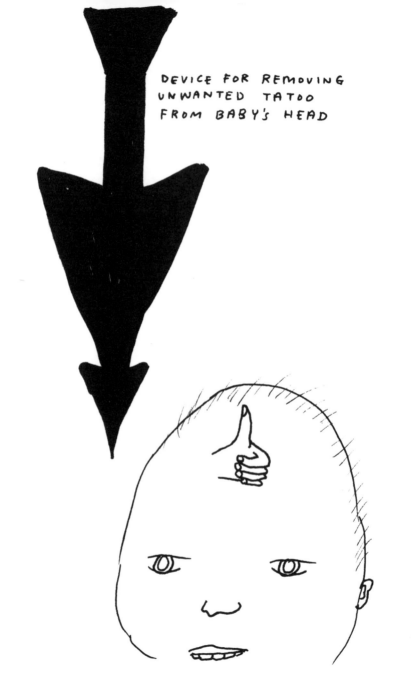

DEVICE FOR REMOVING
UNWANTED TATOO
FROM BABY'S HEAD

THE GIANT

THE
VILLAGE PUB

(THE CHIMNEY IS STICKING UP HIS
ARSE AND HE IS WAITING FOR US TO
LIGHT THE FIRE)

SCIENTISTS INVITED TO PARTY AT
WINDMILL WHERE THEY DIE IN EXPLOSION

I WATCH AS APEMAN
STRANGLES INVISIBLE CHILD

TREE GROWS
IN YOUR
LIKENESS

LIKE YOU, IT BEARS
NO FRUIT AND IS
ALWAYS IN THE WAY

CIVIC SCULPTURE

YOU LOOK
LIKE HAWK
— HAWK LOOKS
LIKE YOU

I BECAME
CONFUSED WHILE
I WAS DRAWING
THE NEST OF TABLES

AND I WAS INTERRUPTED
WHILE I WAS DRAWING
THE VASE OF FLOWERS

AND THE CAT RAN
AWAY WHILE I WAS
TRYING TO DRAW IT

AND I GOT SCARED AS
I DREW THE OLD MAN.
HE WAS SO SINISTER
AND HE TOLD ME FRIGHTENING
STORIES ABOUT HIS BROTHER
WHO WAS ALSO AN ARTIST
UNTIL HE DIED OF A
NERVOUS DISORDER.

- WHAT IS THE NATURE OF THIS DRAWING?

- THIS IS THE BEST DRAWING OF AN ELEPHANT DONE BY A RETARD SO FAR THIS YEAR.

- AND WHAT IS THE MEANING OF THIS DRAWING?

- THE MEANING IS THAT I NOW REGRET DOING IMPERSONATIONS OF THE RETARDS IN MY CARE FOR THE AMUSEMENT OF MY FRIENDS IN THE BAR.

WHAT DO YOU THINK ABOUT WHILE YOU ARE MASTURBATING ?
LADIES
LANDMINES
COMPUTERS
FLOWERS

THOUGHTS OF OTHERS NOT PICTURED ;

    CLOUDS
    FUNGUS
    THE SEA
    CLOCKS

COMPUTER GRAPHICS

SHITE

JOY

AFTER JOY: ARREST, TRIAL,
PRISON, MURDERED IN PRISON.

THIS GARDENER HAS EATEN
POISONOUS BERRIES

THIS GARDENER IS FURIOUS
WITH THE GARDENER WHO HAS
EATEN THE POISONOUS BERRIES

WAR IS POINᵀLESS

IT WILL ONLY LAST AS
LONG AS THE COMBATANTS ARE
ENJOYING THEMSELVES

TROLLS

GOING DOWN THE BOTTOM OF THE GARDEN TO HAVE SEX ON THE COMPOST HEAP.

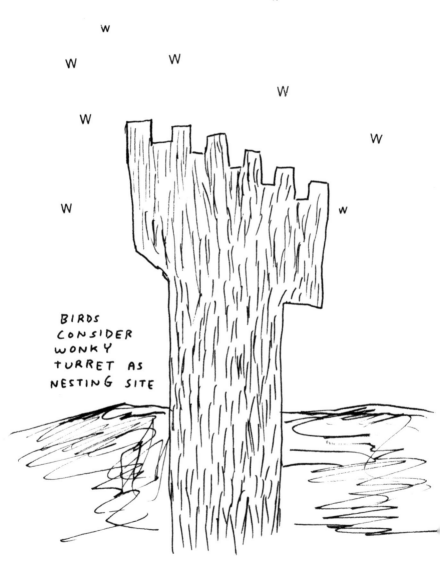

BIRDS
CONSIDER
WONKY
TURRET AS
NESTING SITE

A ROLL OF TAPE

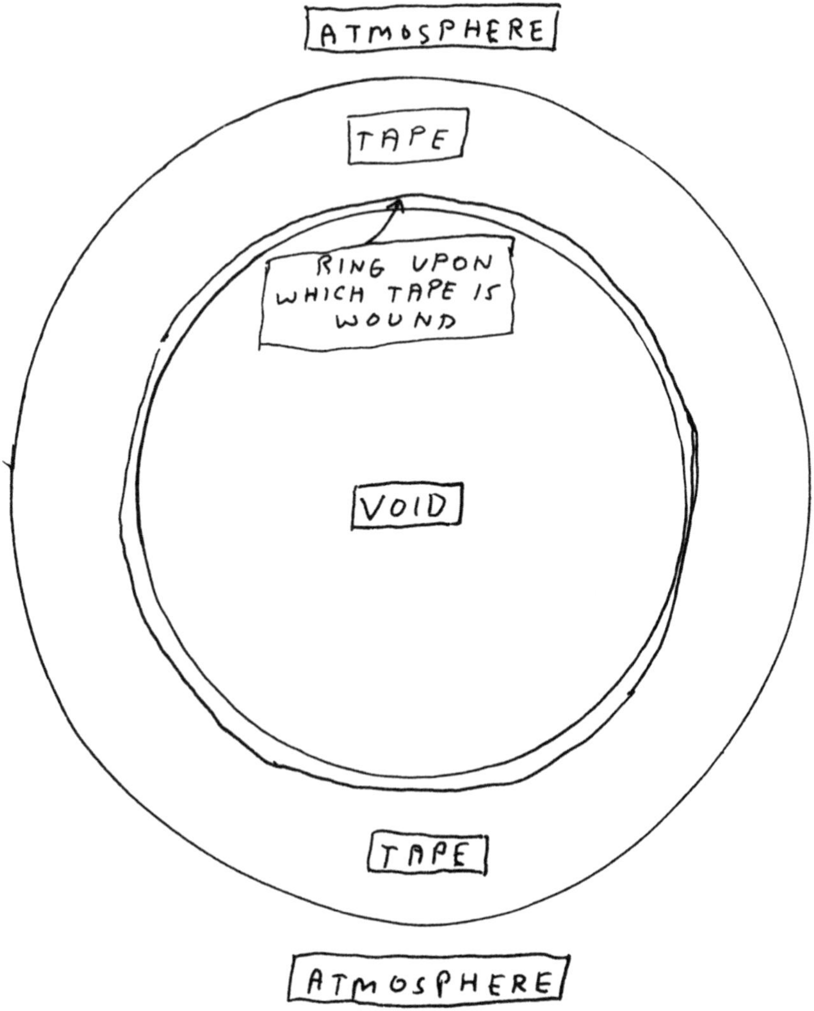

ATMOSPHERE

TAPE

RING UPON
WHICH TAPE IS
WOUND

VOID

TAPE

ATMOSPHERE

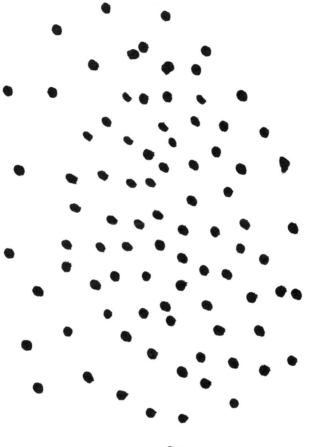

DELICIOUS BLACK CANDY

A.K.A. ▬▬▬▬▬

LICORICE

CRATES

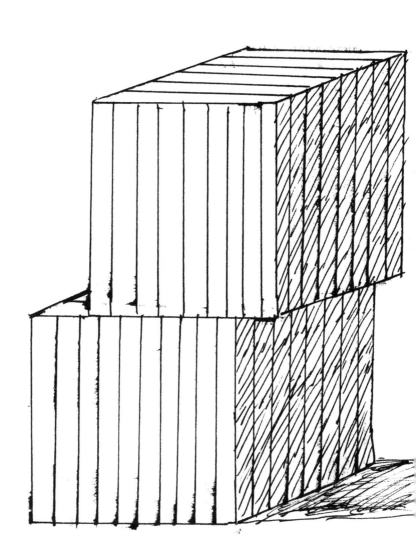

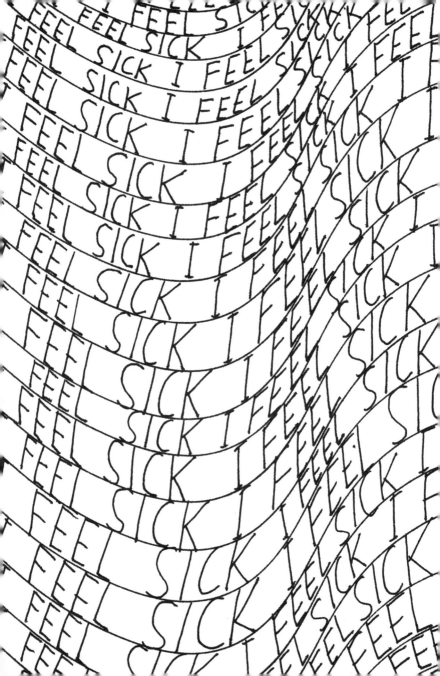

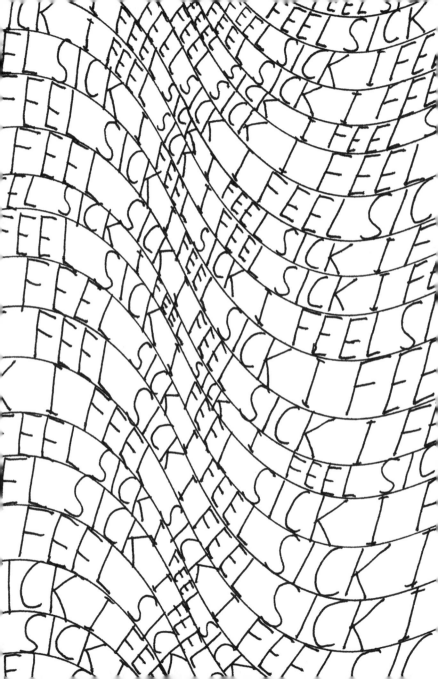

THE SMELL OF FRESHLY BAKED BREAD

MASKS ANOTHER SMELL,
SLIGHTLY UNPLEASENT,
BURNING FLESH MAYBE?
IT'S HARD TO TELL.
LET'S ASK THE BAKER,
BUT WHERE IS THE BAKER?
HAS ANYONE SEEN THE BAKER?

YOU.
(OR IS IT ?,
IT'S HARD TO
TELL AS YOUR
BODY IS ALREADY
HALF-DIGESTED)

IS IT TOO FANCY?

IS IT ~~NOT~~ NOT FANCY ENOUGH?

I CAN MAKE IT LESS FANCY.

OR I CAN MAKE IT MORE FANCY.

OR I CAN SMASH IT TO BITS WITH A HAMMER

OR I CAN SMASH IN YOUR HEAD WITH A HAMMER

THE CHOICE IS YOURS.

BUT IF YOU DO NOT MAKE A CHOICE, I

WILL MAKE A CHOICE ON YOUR BEHALF

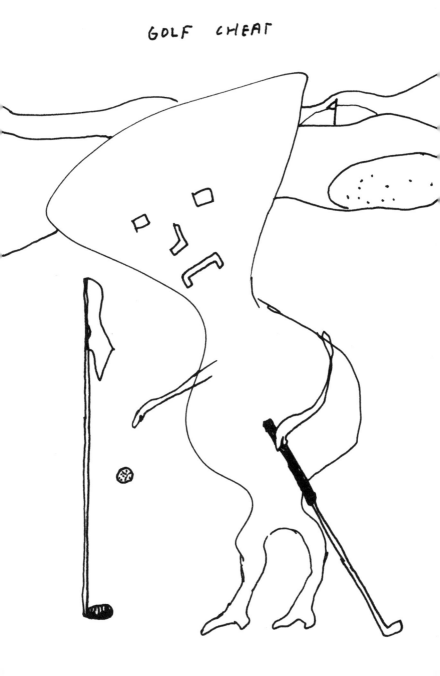

GOLF CHEAT

WHY IS THE WARRIOR DISTRESSED?

— WAR IS OVER

WHAT WOULD MAKE WARRIOR HAPPY ?

ALL   PEOPLE

IN   PRISON

WILL   BE RELEASED
AND   GIVEN WEAPONS

— FAILING THIS:

RESUMPTION OF WAR

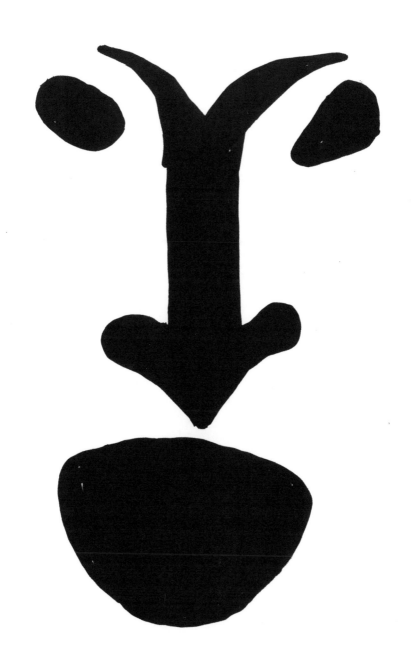

Mystic

Tit

YOU'RE UNHAPPY AREN'T YOU - I CAN TELL

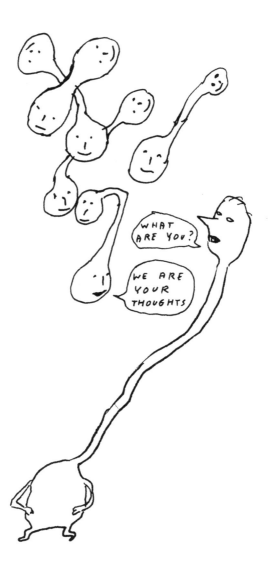

THE ROBOT'S TOUCH

IS TODAY LIGHTER THAN
IT HAS EVER BEEN

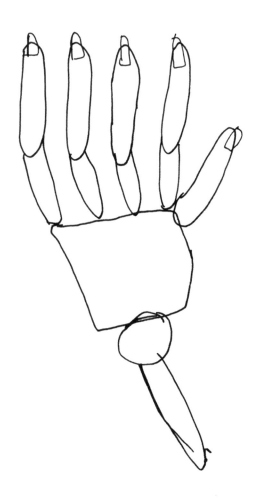

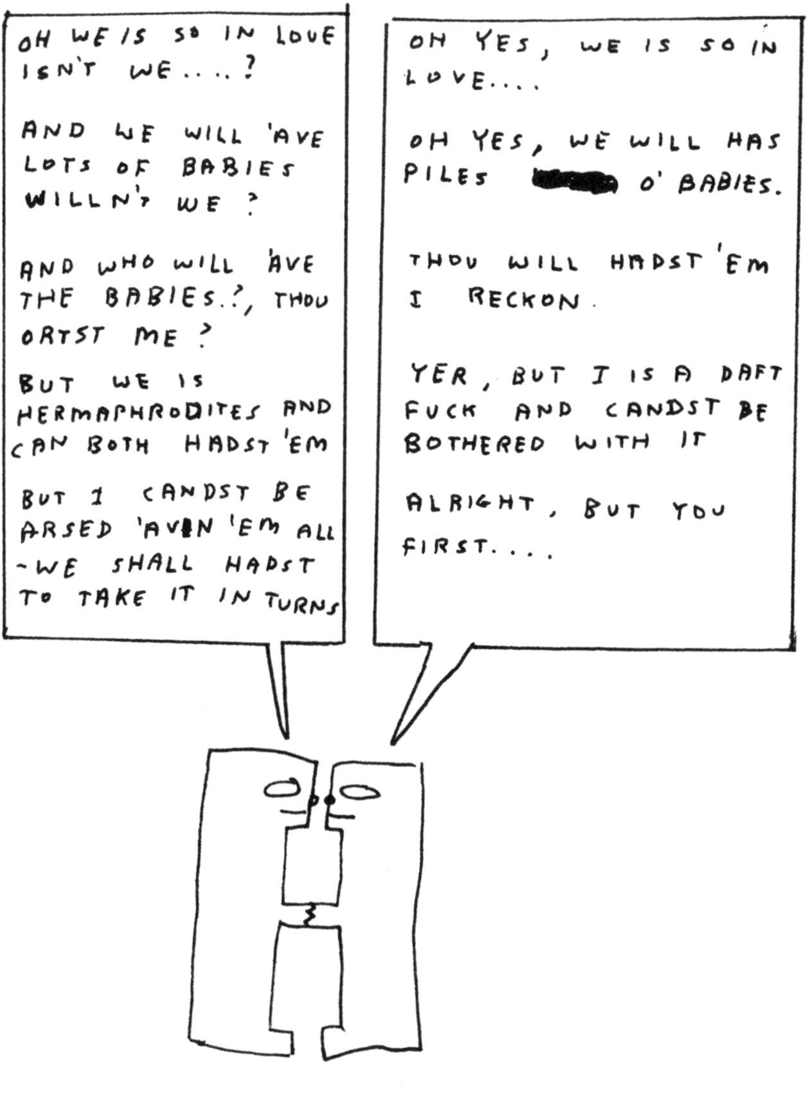

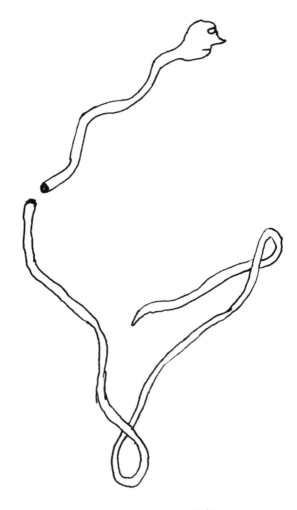

THE DIVIDED SELF

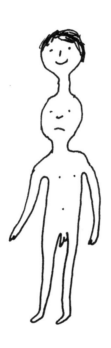

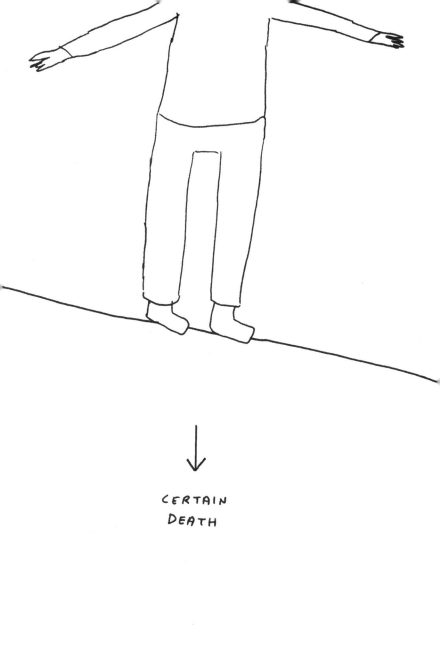

CERTAIN
DEATH

GIANT IDIOT ENTERS GARDEN

GREAT !

WE CAN MAKE HIM CLEAR UP OUR MESS

AND   TURN THE SOIL

AND   DISMANTLE   THE TREE HOUSE

YOU ARE ALTERED WHILST ASLEEP

ME: TODAY I WAS HAMMERING-IN NAILS AND I
CHANCED TO SEE A LITTLE MAN ON THE HEAD
OF ONE OF THE NAILS. HE WAS ONLY
3 MM TALL.

DAD: SO WHAT DID YOU DO?

ME: I SMASHED THE FUCK OUT OF HIM.

DAD: GOOD BOY. I HATE THOSE WEE CUNTS.

A MOMENT IN DRACULA'S LIFE:

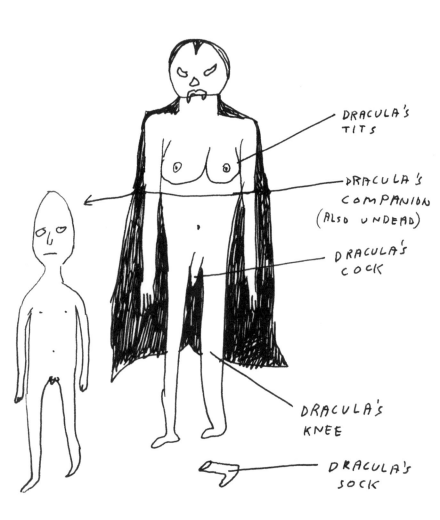

DRACULA'S
TITS

DRACULA'S
COMPANION
(ALSO UNDEAD)

DRACULA'S
COCK

DRACULA'S
KNEE

DRACULA'S
SOCK

THE

PERSON

WOULD YOU STILL LOVE ME
IF I LOOKED LIKE THIS ?
(AND SMELT OF FISH)

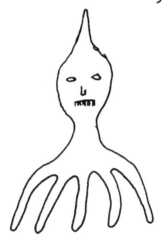

IT WAS THREATENED

BY YOUR HAIRY BACK

THE DYING ARTS:

CONVERSATION :

NOW GENERALLY CONSIDERED
TO BE BORING

ARCHERY :

TOO DIFFICULT

SEX :

STILL POPULAR WITH SOME,
BUT MOST CONSIDER IT
OLD - FASHIONED

STONE - CARVING

TOO DIFFICULT

MAKING VIDEOS

IS   WRONG

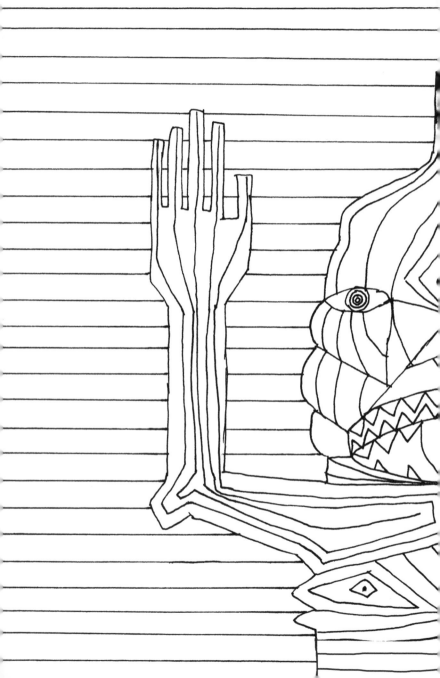

DO NOT LOOK AT THIS IMAGE FOR
TOO LONG. YOU WILL BECOME HYPNOTIZED
AND YOU MIGHT
DRIBBLE ON YOURSELF

ALLOWANCES

BECAUSE YOUR
LIFE IS HORRIBLE,
YOU ARE HORRIBLE
BECAUSE YOU'RE
HORRIBLE
I'M HORRIBLE
AND THIS MEANS MY
GIRLFRIEND IS
HORRIBLE
AND WE'RE HORRIBLE
TO OUR NEIGHBOURS

BUT THEY MAKE ALLOWANCES
FOR US
BECAUSE THEY'VE HEARD ABOUT YOU

TONIGHT IN YOUR DREAMS:

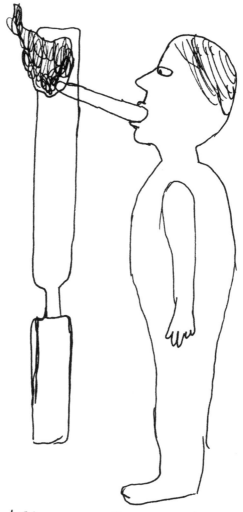

YOU LICK HORSE-SHIT FROM
OFF OF A GIANT SPATULA

HE IS DANCING
TO BRASS BAND MUSIC

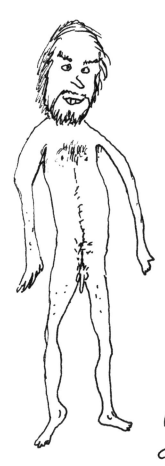

HE IS
DANCING TO
MUSIC OF
MALE -VOICE
CHOIR

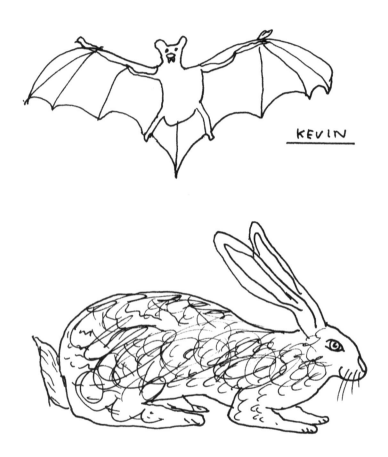

KEVIN

DAVE

DUE TO UNFORSEEN CIRCUMSTANCES TONIGHT'S MATCH WILL GO AHEAD :

PURE & MATHEMATICS

VS.

JOHNNY PLAYING IN THE SAND PIT

THE CONFERENCE

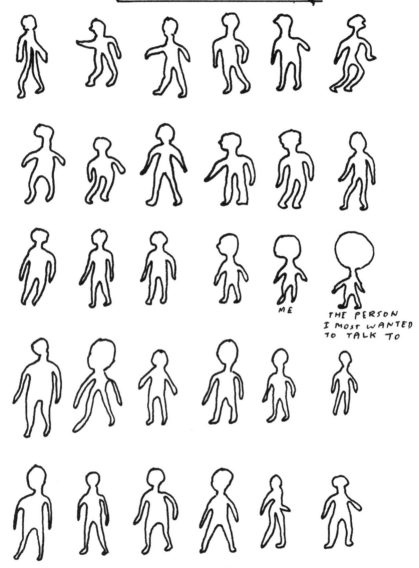

ME

THE PERSON
I MOST WANTED
TO TALK TO

WE SPLIT UP INTO GROUPS OF SIX

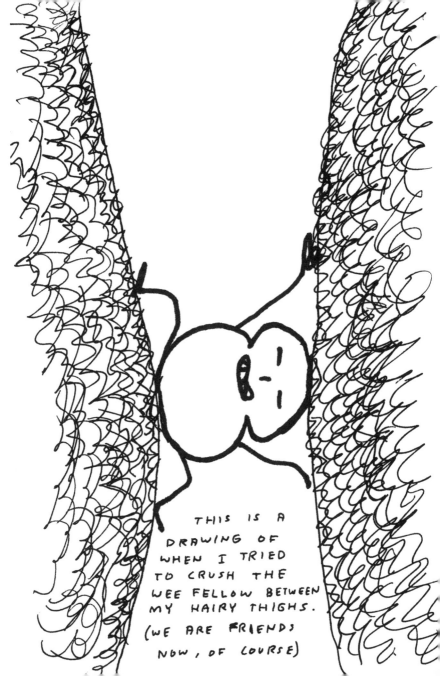

THIS IS A DRAWING OF WHEN I TRIED TO CRUSH THE WEE FELLOW BETWEEN MY HAIRY THIGHS. (WE ARE FRIENDS NOW, OF COURSE)

NOTCHES
ON STICK
INDICATE
SEXUAL CONQUESTS

WHAT'S ON AT THE CINEMA

SCREEN ONE

MICE BEING TORTURED (15)

STARRING GOOFY, DONALD DUCK, ETC

3.30   6.15   9.00   DAILY   LATE SHOW SAT 11.15

SCREEN TWO

THE END OF CIVILIZATION (U)

2.15   4.30   6.30   8.30   DAILY

SCREEN THREE

FILM OF AN OLD MAN TALKING (15)

3.00   6.00   9.00   DAILY

WHAT'S ON AT THE ZOO?

ANIMALS LOOKING BORED, DEPRESSED (U)

CONTINUOUS PERFORMANCE

ANIMALS SHITTING (U)

VARIOUS TIMES

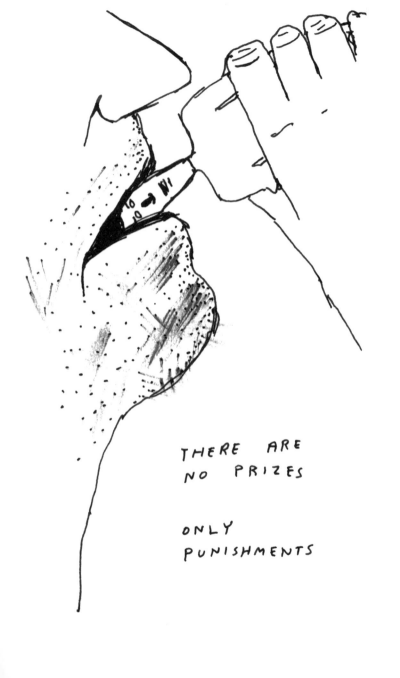

THERE ARE
NO PRIZES

ONLY
PUNISHMENTS

PROGRESS

DO YOU FEAR CHANGE?
WHY SHOULD I FEAR CHANGE? CHANGE IS MY FRIEND
DO YOU FEAR CHAOS?
WHY SHOULD I FEAR CHAOS? A BIT OF A CHAOS NEVER HURT ANYBODY. CHAOS IS THE SPICE OF LIFE
DO YOU FEAR ANARCHY?
ANARCHY? THE SCHOOL HOLIDAYS WOULD LAST FOREVER WITHOUT ANARCHY. THE KIDS LOVE IT.
O.K., TIME'S UP....
ALREADY?
YES. SAME TIME NEXT WEEK?
YES, THANK-YOU DOCTOR.

SKULLS

SKULL OF FUCK KNOWS WHAT

SKULL OF
BORIS KARLOFF
(V. SCARY)

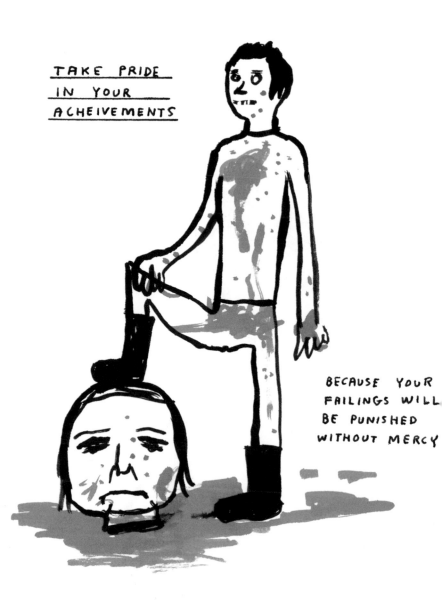

TAKE PRIDE
IN YOUR
ACHEIVEMENTS

BECAUSE YOUR
FAILINGS WILL
BE PUNISHED
WITHOUT MERCY

WEDDING CEREMONY

"DO YOU, RAMBO, TAKE THE CREATURE
PICTURED OPPOSITE TO BE YOUR
LAWFULLY - WEDDED WIFE"

WE WENT TO SEE A PERFORMANCE
EVERYONE THOUGHT IT WAS BRILLIANT
EXCEPT US
WE THOUGHT IT WAS CRAP

GIANT PREYING MANTIS IN HIS NATURAL HABITAT

GIANT PREYING MANTIS IN THE
CONTROLLED ENVIRONMENT OF THE
LABORATORY (WITH FRIEND)

SPECIAL SELECTION
100 %

MADE FROM OLD
SLEEPING BAGS
THAT TRAMPS HAVE DIED IN

Really stinks

— WOULD YOU LIKE A BITE OF MY MOUNTAIN?

— NO THANKS.

— DON'T BE SO POLITE. HAVE A BITE; IT'S
DELICIOUS. HAVE THE SUMMIT IF YOU LIKE.
GO ON — I CAN SEE YOU LOOKING AT IT, YOU
WANT SOME DON'T YOU?

— I WASN'T LOOKING AT YOUR MOUNTAIN, I WAS
LOOKING AT THE CLIMBERS THERE ON THE
NORTH FACE. AND THE SHERPAS AND THEIR
BEASTS OF BURDEN.

— OH YES. HAVE THEM BY ALL MEANS.

— THANK YOU. MMMMM, THEY'RE REALLY TASTY.

— I THINK YOU HAVE A YAK STUCK IN YOUR
TEETH.

DIFFICULT PENANCE:

TRANSCRIBE

BIBLE   IN

THE MOTORCYCLE COURIER HAS ARRIVED
HE HAS BROUGHT YOU YOUR VALLIUM

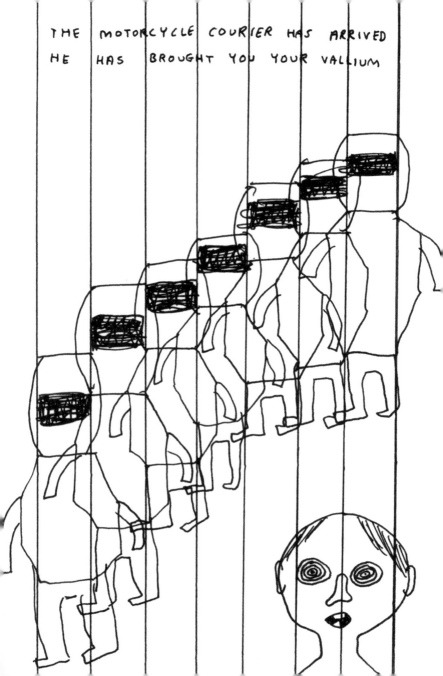

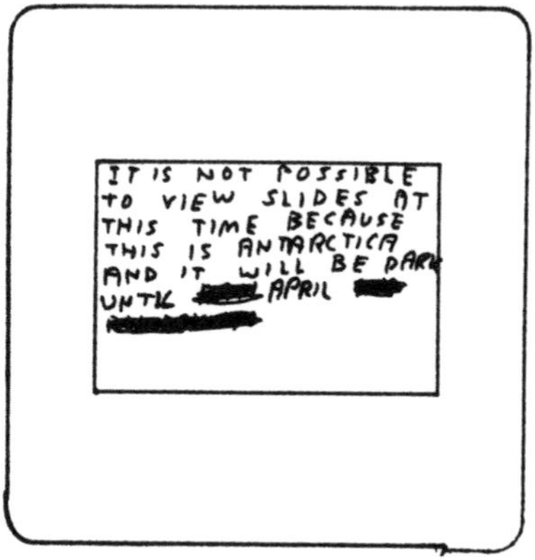

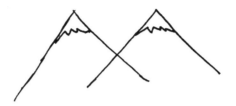

WHEN YOU CAN SEE
THE ~~------~~ TWO MOUNTAINS
AS ONE YOU CAN
START TO CLIMB IT

STORMY WEATHER

THE MUSIC OF THE VACCUM CLEANER

AND MAKE THE SHAPE OF A CUNT

EVIL THINKER

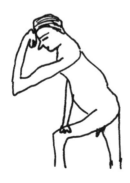

JUMPING THROUGH HOOPS:

TREVOR SUCCESFULLY ~~━~~ JUMPS THROUGH THE HOOP.

TREVOR'S DOG TRIES TO JUMP THROUGH THE HOOP BUT FAILS

TREVOR'S DOG IS GIVEN A LETHAL INJECTION

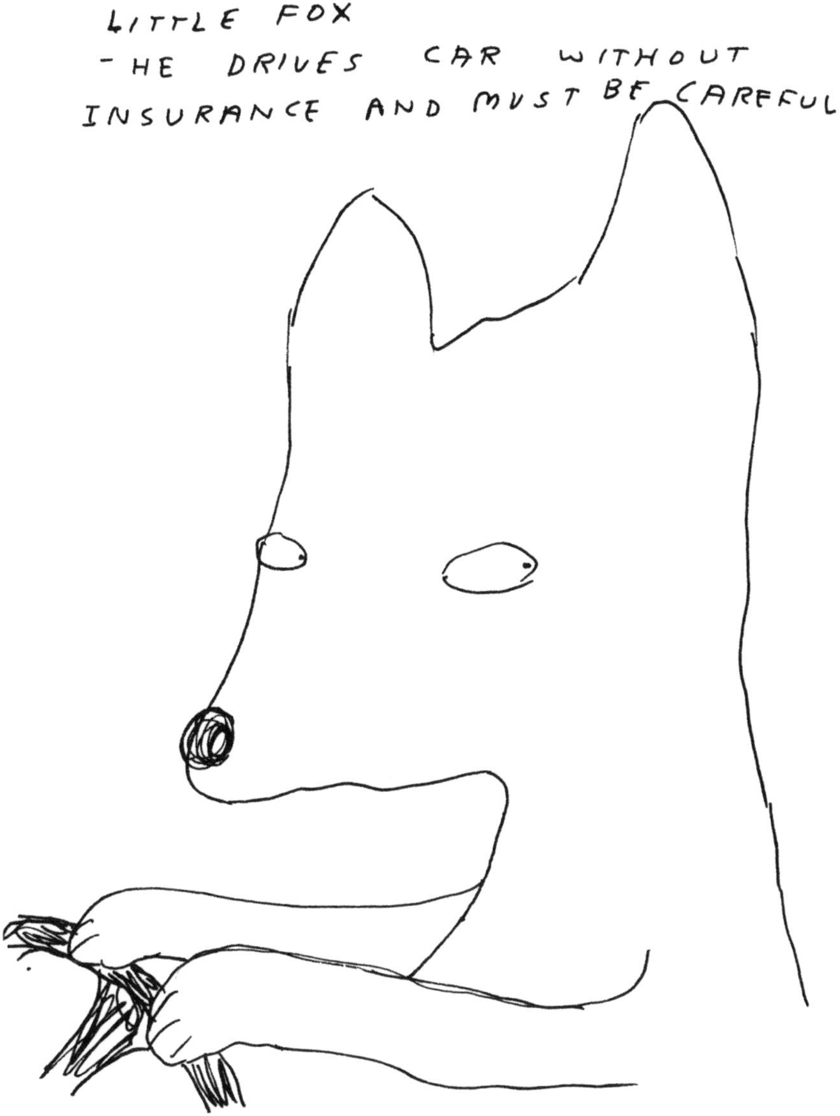

LITTLE FOX
- HE DRIVES CAR WITHOUT
INSURANCE AND MUST BE CAREFUL

PLEASE
TRY TO
BE QUIET

(WE DON'T WANT
HIM TO KNOW WE
ARE WATCHING)

SUCCESS HASN'T 'CHANGED HIM'

BUT STILL HE LOOKS DIFFERENT

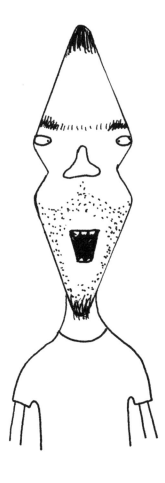

BATS

TWATS

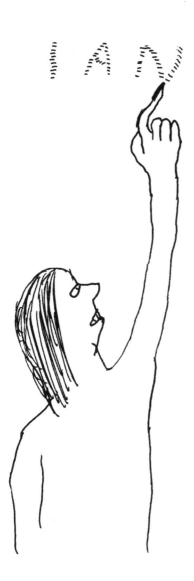

IAN SCRATCHES
HIS NAME

Q. WHAT ARE THEY BURNING
IN THE FURNACE TODAY?

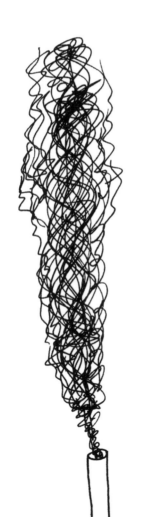

A. PROOF OF YOUR
EXISTENCE.

BUYING A NEW CAR

- WHAT KIND OF CAR ARE YOU GOING TO BUY?
- I AM GOING TO BUY A ~~██████ ████~~
  PRINCE ANDREW SUCKED MY COCK, YOU
  KNOW 1·8 L .
- I DON'T KNOW MUCH ABOUT CARS; IS
  THAT THE MAKE OR THE MODEL?
- THAT'S THE MODEL. IT IS MADE BY
  BADGER IS PARANOID ABOUT COLLAPSING
  TUNNELS.
- AND IF YOU CAN'T BUY THAT PARTICULAR
  CAR WILL YOU BUY A DIFFERENT ONE?
- IF I CAN'T GET A PRINCE ANDREW
  SUCKED MY COCK, YOU KNOW 1·8L,
  THEN I'LL GO FOR A PRINCE ANDREW
  SUCKED MY COCK, YOU KNOW 1·6 L,
  WHICH IS ESSENTIALLY THE SAME CAR
  WITH A SMALLER ENGINE.
- AND WHAT COLOUR WITH YOU CHOOSE?
- I'LL GO FOR CHEMICAL TOILET,
- WHAT COLOUR IS THAT?
- IT'S A KIND OF METALLIC 'BATTLESHIP
  GREY'. MY YACHT IS ALSO THAT COLOUR.
- AND WHAT KIND OF YACHT DO YOU HAVE?
-

        ETC. . . .

SLOW LEARNER :

THE FURNACE ASSISTANT

EVIL

SATAN DEPARTS,
HAVING TOLD ROBERT
AN AMUSING STORY.

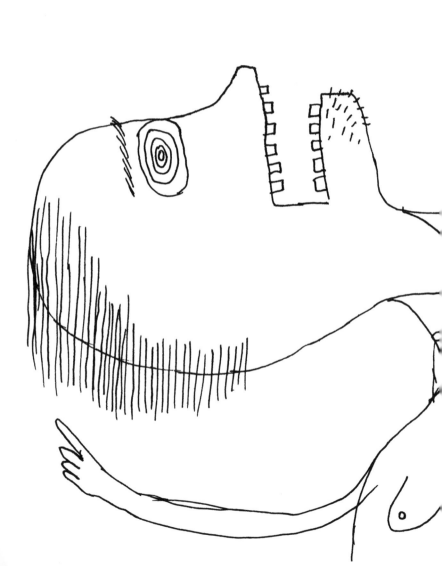

DO NOT LOOK AT THIS IMAGE FOR TOO LONG YOU WILL BECOME CONFUSED AND YOU MIGHT START TO TALK NONSENSE

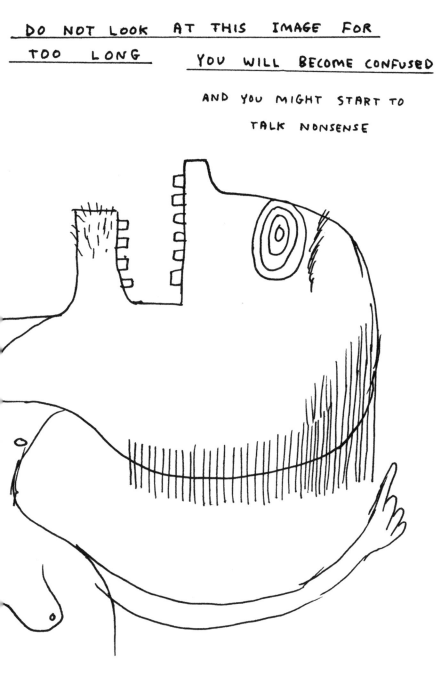

I ♡ GRIM REALITY
AND CHARLTON HESTON

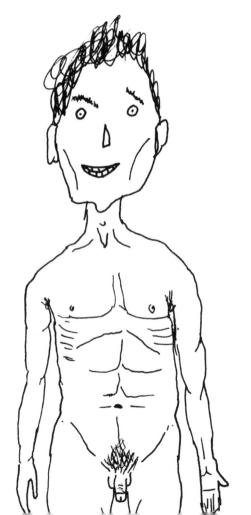

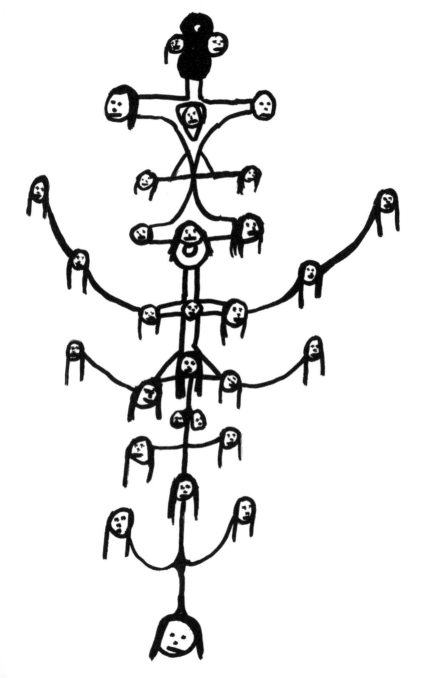

EVIL LEGS
EVIL ARMS
EVIL EARS
EVIL EYES
EVIL HANDS
EVIL JUMPER
EVIL WRISTWATCH
EVIL TROUSERS
EVIL SUNGLASSES
EVIL PHOTOCOPIER
EVIL MOUNTAIN BIKE
EVIL SWIMMING POOL
EVIL WOMAN WHO WORKS AT SWIMMING POOL
EVIL SWIMMING TRUNKS
EVIL WATER WINGS
EVIL CHILDREN
EVIL SHOWER
EVIL CAN OF 7 UP
EVIL WALK HOME
EVIL MOTHER
EVIL FISH FINGERS
EVIL T.V.
EVIL COCOA
EVIL BED
EVIL DREAMS
EVIL AWAKENING
EVIL BREAKFAST
EVIL PAPER ROUND
EVIL SCHOOL
EVIL MATHS
EVIL MATHS TEACHER
EVIL MACHETE
EVIL BITS OF EVIL MATHS TEACHER

Q. WHAT IS YOUR INTENT FOR THE TENT ?

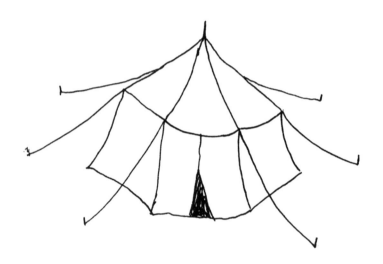

A. MY INTENT FOR THE TENT IS THAT A SMALLER TENT BE PITCHED INSIDE IT.

Q. AND WHAT IS YOUR INTENT FOR THE TENT INSIDE THE TENT?

A. ~~MY INTENT~~ MY INTENT FOR THE TENT INSIDE THE TENT IS THAT A SMALLER TENT BE PITCHED INSIDE IT.

Q. AND WHAT IS YOUR INTENT FOR THE TENT INSIDE THE TENT INSIDE THE TENT?

A. MY INTENT FOR THE TENT INSIDE THE TENT INSIDE THE TENT IS TO PITCH A SMALLER TENT INSIDE IT.

Q. AND WHAT IS YOUR INTENT FOR THE TENT INSIDE THE TENT INSIDE THE TENT INSIDE THE TENT?

A. I AM GOING TO SPEND MY HOLIDAY INSIDE IT.

Q. WHY?

A. BECAUSE IT WILL BE UNLIKELY TO LEAK. AND BECAUSE THE BITING INSECTS WILL NOT BE ABLE TO GET AT ME. THE BITING INSECTS RUINED MY HOLIDAY LAST YEAR. I WAS COVERED IN BITES. MILLIONS OF BITES. I LOOKED LIKE I HAD THE POX.

1. WHY ARE YOU CRYING?

THERE ARE IMAGES OF STARVING CHILDREN ON THE T.V.

2. WHY ARE YOU CRYING NOW?

THE T.V. QUIZ CONTESTANT HAS JUST FAILED IN HER ATTEMPT TO WIN ~~£~~ £1 MILLION

3. AND WHY ARE YOU CRYING NOW?

THERE ARE IMAGES OF BEAUTIFUL THINGS WHICH I CANNOT AFFORD TO BUY

4. WHY ARE YOU SILENT?

I AM PREPARING TO MASTURBATE

PLEASE DON'T LET THEM DIE

KEEP THEM
ALIVE SO
THEY CAN BE
TORTURED

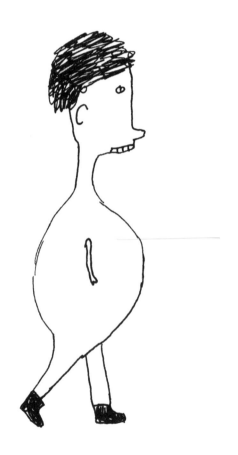

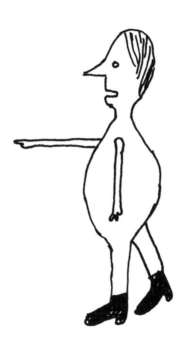

DESIGN FOR MOUSETRAP

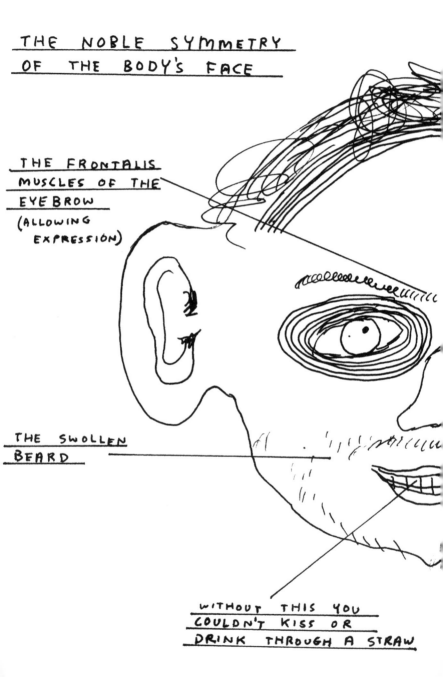

THE NOBLE SYMMETRY
OF THE BODY'S FACE

THE FRONTALIS MUSCLES OF THE EYEBROW
(ALLOWING EXPRESSION)

THE SWOLLEN BEARD

WITHOUT THIS YOU COULDN'T KISS OR DRINK THROUGH A STRAW

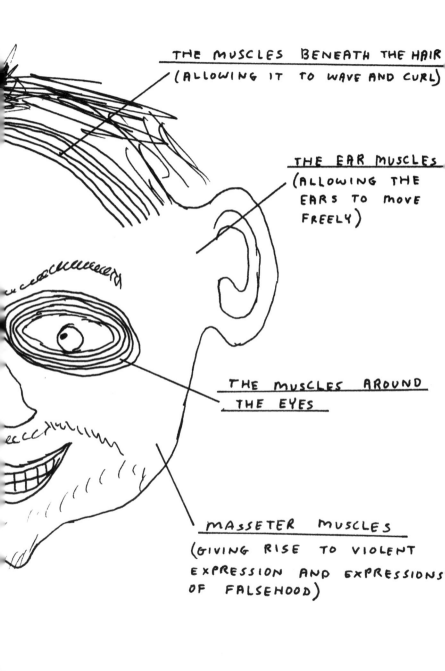

THE MUSCLES BENEATH THE HAIR
(ALLOWING IT TO WAVE AND CURL)

THE EAR MUSCLES
(ALLOWING THE
EARS TO MOVE
FREELY)

THE MUSCLES AROUND
THE EYES

MASSETER MUSCLES
(GIVING RISE TO VIOLENT
EXPRESSION AND EXPRESSIONS
OF FALSEHOOD)

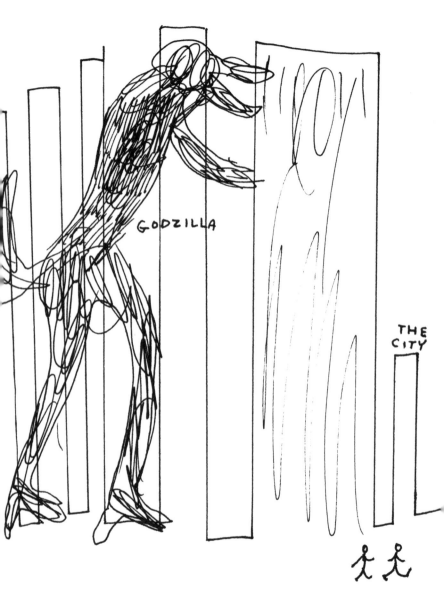

GODZILLA

THE CITY

OUTER SPACE

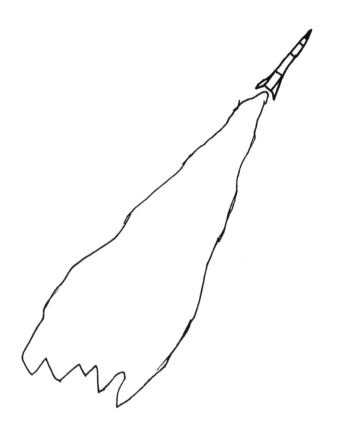

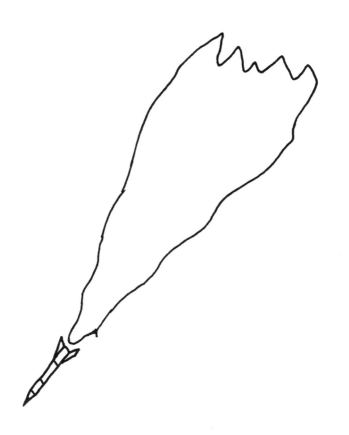

IS RUBBISH

COFFEE

COFFEE IS POISON

DOUGHNUT

DOUGHNUTS ARE POISON

THESE BIRDS ARE FUCKED-UP
FROM EATING POISONED
WORMS AND NOW THEY'RE
TRYING TO BUILD A NEST
OUT OF SHARP BITS OF WIRE

FOX LICKS MAGIC STUMP

WHAT DISTRESSES ME

WHAT DISTRESSES ME IS THAT EVEN
THE SMOOTHEST OF OBJECTS IS INCREDIBLY
ROUGH AND BUMPY WHEN VIEWED THROUGH
A POWERFUL MICROSCOPE. WHEN I THINK
OF IT I AM FILLED WITH DESPAIR.

I AM
WOKEN EACH
MORNING BY
THE SOUND OF
BIRDS COUGHING

THEN

NOW

THE LESS-VISIBLE MAN

HE'S NOT INVISIBLE, HE'S JUST LESS-VISIBLE.

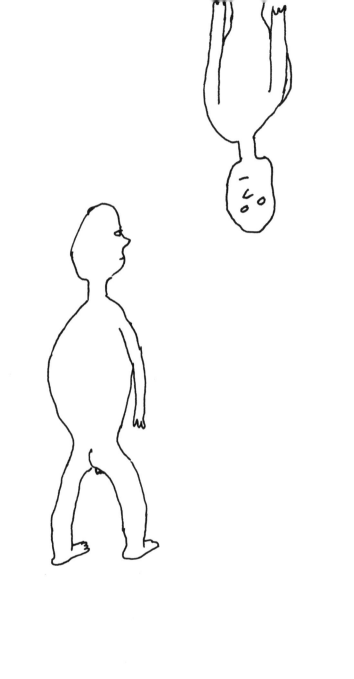

GRATER ALTERS FORM

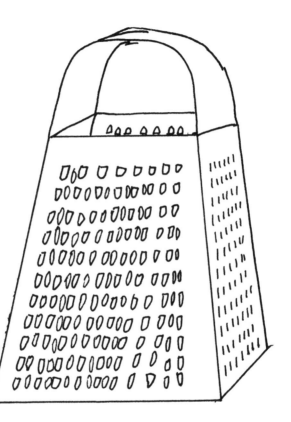

FORM OF HUMAN SKULL
ALTERED THRU' GRATING

FARMERS

NORMAL
FARMER

RETARDED
FARMER

WE WERE FEARFUL OF YOU

THEN WE REALISED WE HAD

NOTHING TO FEAR

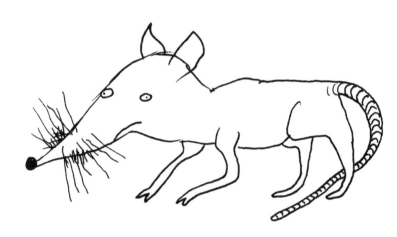

AND WE POISONED YOU

THE PAWNS

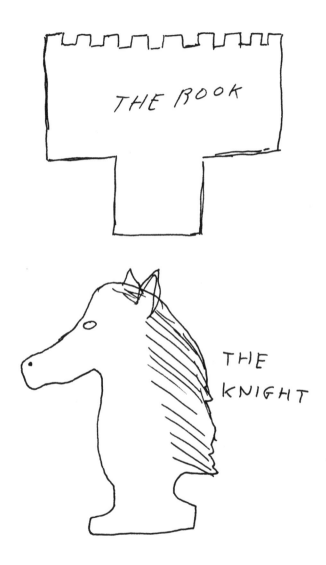

THE ROOK

THE KNIGHT

YOUR NEW JOB:

TO COLLECT FARTS IN A JAR

THEN YOU GET MADE REDUNDANT
AND YOU GET A NEW JOB:

TO PICK THE BITS OFF THINGS;
   EG: DOG HAIRS OFF SOFA
          POPPY SEEDS OFF CARPET
          FLEAS OFF DOG
          FLUFF OFF RUNWAY

THEN YOU GET MADE REDUNDANT AGAIN
AND YOU GET ANOTHER NEW JOB:

TO FIND LOST CONTACT LENS IN AUSTRALIAN
OUTBACK.

YOU DO THIS FOR TEN YEARS OR SO
AND THEN YOU GET A BETTER JOB;

HAVING DRUGS TESTED ON YOU AT
THE INSANE ASYLUM

THEN YOU RETIRE TO CONCENTRATE ON
YOUR TRUE PASSION IN LIFE;

DATA ENTRY

2 SECONDS FLAT:

YOU DRINK GARDEN POND
(WATER, PLANT & FISH LIFE, ROCKS)